P

*Imitating What's Contained*
*Obtaining What's Promised*

*(A companion to The Scriptural Rosary)*

by

Patrick Yanke

www.yankeacademy.com

*ISBN: 978-0-578-92576-9*

Excerpts from the
*New American Bible, Revised Edition*
and the
*Catechism of the Catholic Church (CCC)*
except where noted

*Foreword by*

*His Excellency*
*Joseph E. Strickland*
*Bishop of the Diocese of Tyler, TX*

*Printed in the USA by*
*AlphaGraphics of Downtown Raleigh, NC*

I am pleased to be able to offer this Foreword for Patrick Yanke's book, "The Personal Rosary". Praying the Rosary has become a dynamic part of my prayer life in the last several years that continues to develop and grow. The title Patrick has chosen for his book on the Rosary is very descriptive and to my mind very important. It evokes two dimensions of "personal" that I believe are essential if we wish to pray the Rosary in the way Our Blessed Mother and her Son Jesus Christ want it to be incorporated into our faith journey.

The first dimension is that the Rosary is personal because it is about a person, Jesus Christ. At its very core the Rosary is a reflection on the whole mystery of Jesus Christ, God's Divine Son as He has become incarnate among us. I love to approach the mysteries following the chronology of Jesus's life from His conception in the first Joyful Mystery to the hidden years to the first Luminous Mystery where Our Lord is baptized by John the Baptist. His incarnate journey continues with His Passion in the Sorrowful Mysteries and the after His death we reflect on the Glorious Mysteries of His Resurrection and return to the

Father. Jesus Christ is the person at the heart of the Rosary with the Blessed Virgin Mary at His side throughout the journey. Patrick's personal rosary helps put us more intimately in relationship with our Beloved Savior and Lord.

The second dimension that "The Personal Rosary" helps to evoke is the reality of the individual person praying the mysteries. In this sense the Rosary is personal because it is an intimate encounter between one son or daughter of God and the divine mysteries that God has revealed to us through His Son Jesus. When we pray the Rosary we bring ourselves before the mysteries of Jesus Christ as we are and as personal beings we are different every time we approach this meditation of the mysteries of our faith. At times praying the Joyful Mysteries or the Sorrowful Mysteries may resonate deeply with where we are on our personal journey in the moment. At other times praying the Luminous Mysteries or the Glorious Mysteries may be in sharp contrast with our personal feelings at that moment. Whatever the specific interplay may be between our lives and the mysteries of Jesus Christ, the encounter is always personal.

# FOREWORD

I pray that many may embrace Patrick's book as an opportunity to explore more deeply their own personal relationship with Jesus Christ as they ponder the reflections Patrick shares in "The Personal Rosary".

Bishop Joseph E. Strickland
Diocese of Tyler, TX

"There are not one hundred people in the United States who hate The Catholic Church, but there are millions who hate what they wrongly perceive the Catholic Church to be."

- Archbishop Fulton J. Sheen

## Why a Personal Rosary?

In the Rosary, we meditate on the mysteries of Christ and His mother. The Virgin Mary shares in the joy of His coming and the suffering of His passion and death. She is present in the major moments of His life and was raised to join Him in glory at her passing. The Rosary is a reflection on His life in Scripture, her life of absolute faithfulness, and our own lives imitating them in communion with His Bride, the Church.

This book is a collection of prayers for deeper meditation on living the mysteries in our own lives. Where *The Scriptural Rosary* follows the life of Christ in Scripture, *The Personal Rosary* meditates on our lives following Him. As we pray to "*imitate what [these mysteries] contain*", we focus our meditation on how we can take up our crosses in daily sacrificial love for God and one another.

*We must continue to accomplish in ourselves the stages of Jesus' life and His mysteries and often to beg Him to perfect and realize them in us and in His whole Church. . . For it is the plan of the Son of God to make us and the whole Church partake in His mysteries and to extend them to and continue them in us and in*

*His whole Church. This is His plan for fulfilling His mysteries in us* (CCC 521 [St John Eudes, LH, Week 33, Friday, OR]).

*"Ignorance of Scripture is ignorance of Christ"* (St Jerome).

*"In reading the Catechism of the Catholic Church we can perceive the wonderful unity of the mystery of God..."* (Pope John Paul II).

In Christ, we see a dual nature; both divine and human. In our prayers, we call on those natures as we pray in supplication to His Godhead and reflect on His life lived among us. It isn't enough that He forgives us—we are to forgive. It isn't enough that He took up His cross—we must take up ours and follow Him. We are *filling up what is lacking in the afflictions of Christ* (Col 1:24) as we, His mystical Body, carry on His mission to call all people to Himself through lives of sacrificial love.

As human beings with immortal souls made in the image and likeness of God, we are called to participate in the divine life through grace. While He is able to enter His creation and become one of us, we have no capacity to enter His nature on our own. The infinite can take on the nature of the finite but we finite beings cannot grasp infinity. He became like us to make us like Him... but we have a role to play —following where He leads us. As He reaches down to pull us up, we must reach up to take His hand in cooperation with His plan for us (Jer 29:11).

He doesn't need us. We need Him. When we glorify Him with our praise, we haven't changed His level of glory. We have oriented our worship to Him who alone is worthy of our praise. He demonstrates the depth of His love for us by coming when we were at our worst to suffer abuse and death at our hands so that we might be lifted up to join Him forever in Heaven. It's a love we can't truly fathom—only hope to imitate.

The love we share is both vertical and horizontal. In the greatest commandment, we love God first and then our neighbor as ourselves. In the Ten Commandments, the first three are devoted to our relationship with God and the other seven to our relationship with our fellow men. Just so in the Rosary do we reflect on God in the person of Jesus in *The Scriptural Rosary* and on our lives lived in imitation of Him in *The Personal Rosary*.

## Prayer

Begin and end with the sign of the Cross—the sign of Christ's love for us.

The Church teaches us that perfect prayer includes four main elements; adoration, contrition, thanksgiving, and supplication (ACTS). We find all of these in our Lord's Prayer in the words He gave us. What's fascinating is the realization that we are emotional creatures... and our main emotions may be categorized into four: joy, anger, sadness, and fear. The God who created us engages us in prayer. In joy, we adore Him. Overcoming anger, we forgive and are forgiven. We rise from sadness in gratitude. We banish fear by turning to God for help. As emotional, praying children, we adore, forgive, thank, and trust…

*Our Father, Who art in Heaven, hallowed be thy name. Thy kingdom come. Thy will be done on Earth as it is in Heaven* (**adoration**)

*Give us this day, our daily bread.* (**thanksgiving**)

*Forgive us our trespasses as we forgive those who trespass against us.* (**contrition**)

*Lead us not into temptation but deliver us from evil.* (**supplication**)

God doesn't need our prayers. Our prayers do not change Him. In love, He desires to enter into communion with us. Prayer changes us as we turn to Him who is the author of life and we orient our will to His. Prayer humbles us to decrease our prideful hearts that He may increase love for His will in us (John 3:30-36). The God who loves us so much that He willed us into being and gave His life to save us calls us to prayer—to be focused on Him who fashioned each of us with purpose.

The Hail Mary is a reflection on the mother of our Lord whose purpose is divine motherhood. She is first among Christians and close to the Sacred Heart of Jesus. She was with Him at the major moments of His earthly life and is alive with Him now—sharing in His glory in Heaven. We approach her with the words of Heaven spoken reverently by the Angel (Luke 1:28), recount her Canticle (Luke 1:48) and as the mother of Christ and His mystical Body (the Church… you and me) we ask her to pray for us.

What better way is there for us to be changed than to be conformed to Christ's perfect filial obedience and emulate Mary's life of perfect faithfulness?

## The Rosary

Prayer isn't always about the words we say, but rather the spirit and heart we bring to our prayers (CCC 2562). The words may change when we approach His throne of mercy and grace but not the spirit behind the words. In the Rosary, the main prayers are important elements but our focus is on the mysteries we contemplate. Touching the beads, our attention is not just on the repetition of our words but deep in meditation on the mysteries before us. We engage all of our senses. May the reflections given with each mystery help deepen an understanding of the life of Christ in each of us.

In the model of *The Scriptural Rosary*, the reflections may be meditated on with each bead of the Rosary or one reflection may be chosen for meditation through each mystery (useful when it isn't practical to read along). Just as the reflections are meant to be personal, so is the method used for meditation. Living the mysteries of Christ is as uniquely personal as each individual. The reflections given here are a suggested beginning. From this beginning, the meditations will likely lead to deeper and more individually intimate contemplation.

The original mysteries of the Rosary are fairly simple to engage on a personal level. At the heart of each is the creed we profess. In the Joyful Mysteries, our Lord enters the world. The Sorrowful Mysteries explore His passion and death. The Glorious Mysteries deal with resurrection and eternity. All of us will experience these things to some degree and we can relate to them fairly easily.

The Luminous Mysteries can be harder to relate and imitate... on the surface. We can't generally change water to wine or shine like the Sun. However, delving deeper into the mysteries, we find that the Luminous Mysteries remind us who Christ is. They powerfully illuminate His identity... and our own in communion with Him. They don't tell a narrative story—they paint a picture.

The mysteries of the Rosary may meet us on an emotional level. In most of our daily choices, we are presented an opportunity to express love or fear. In love, we are **joyful**—selfless and giving; in fear, we are selfish and reserved. Love drives us forward; fear is paralyzing and holds us back. Love seeks what is best for others; in fear, we are concerned with what we have to lose. Love requires action, not just feeling (James 1:22); fear is suffocating.

The first step in moving from fear to love is **trust**—trusting in the goodness and mercy of God. When our fear manifests as anger, the antidote is **forgiveness**. When fear causes sorrow, the solution is **gratitude**—it's hard to be sorrowful and grateful at the same time.

In the Joyful Mysteries, we can reflect in **gratitude** on the God who personally came into the world to save us. In the Luminous Mysteries, we can learn to **trust** in our identity as children of God—made in His image and likeness, reborn in Baptism. In the Sorrowful Mysteries, we reflect on **forgiveness** and pray for the grace to forgive those who persecute us. The Glorious Mysteries are a reflection on the everlasting **joy** to come in the eternal Kingdom of God.

Our journey of faith is also modeled in the progression of the mysteries of the Rosary. We are **joyful** when experiencing God's call (Acts 8:36-39). Our path and His will are **illuminated** in contemplation of His revelation (Rom 8:14). We experience **sorrow** on our journey (2 Tim 3:12). Beyond the sorrows of this world, God's way leads to **glory** (Rev 3:5). As we **imitate** the mysteries of Christ, the world yields abuse and rejection. We wait in joyful hope to **obtain** the promises of our loving and faithful Father.

Prayer is essential to a life of faith (CCC 2744). We should pray without ceasing (CCC 2742). As part of a life of prayer, the Rosary is a deep meditation of learning to love—following Him who is life-giving love personified. Contemplation of the mysteries of the Rosary is a reflection on the life and love of Christ who came to give His life as ransom for ours.

May the grace of our Lord Jesus Christ, the love of God, and the communion of the Holy Spirit be with us as we pray—patiently traveling through this valley of tears—joyfully awaiting His coming in glory.

The Holy Father suggests the recitation of the Rosary as follows:

JOYFUL mysteries on Monday and Saturday
LUMINOUS on Thursday
SORROWFUL on Tuesday and Friday
GLORIOUS on Wednesday and Sunday

with this exception:

JOYFUL mysteries on Sundays of the Christmas season
SORROWFUL mysteries on Sundays of Lent

The Mysteries:

Resources:

## The Apostles' Creed

I believe in God, the Father almighty,
Creator of heaven and earth,
and in Jesus Christ, his only Son, our Lord,
who was conceived by the Holy Spirit,
born of the Virgin Mary,
suffered under Pontius Pilate,
was crucified, died and was buried;
he descended into hell;
on the third day he rose again from the dead;
he ascended into heaven, and is seated at the
right hand of God the Father almighty;
from there he will come
to judge the living and the dead.
I believe in the Holy Spirit,
the holy catholic Church,
the communion of saints,
the forgiveness of sins,
the resurrection of the body,
and life everlasting.
Amen.

## The Lord's Prayer

Our Father,
Who art in heaven,
hallowed be Thy name;
Thy kingdom come;
Thy will be done on earth as it is in Heaven.
Give us this day our daily bread; and
forgive us our trespasses
as we forgive those who trespass against us;
and lead us not into temptation,
but deliver us from evil. Amen.

## Hail Mary

Hail Mary, full of grace.
The Lord is with thee.
Blessed art thou among women,
and blessed is the fruit of thy womb, Jesus.
Holy Mary, Mother of God, pray for us sinners,
now and at the hour of our death.
Amen.

## Glory Be (Doxology)

Glory be to the Father,
to the Son, and
to the Holy Spirit,
as it was, is now, and
ever shall be, world without end.
Amen.

## Fatima Prayer
(Often said after the Glory Be)

O my Jesus, forgive us our sins,
save us from the fires of Hell;
lead all souls to Heaven,
especially those who have
most need of your mercy.

# THE PERSONAL ROSARY

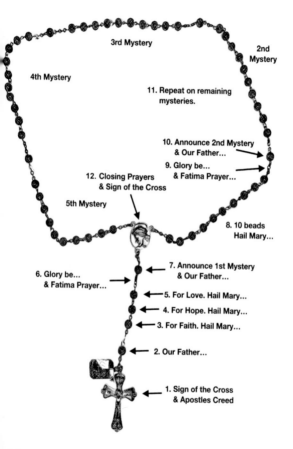

3rd Mystery

2nd Mystery

4th Mystery

11. Repeat on remaining mysteries.

10. Announce 2nd Mystery & Our Father...

9. Glory be... & Fatima Prayer...

12. Closing Prayers & Sign of the Cross

5th Mystery

8. 10 beads Hail Mary...

7. Announce 1st Mystery & Our Father...

6. Glory be... & Fatima Prayer...

5. For Love. Hail Mary...

4. For Hope. Hail Mary...

3. For Faith. Hail Mary...

2. Our Father...

1. Sign of the Cross & Apostles Creed

14

# The
# Joyful Mysteries

*Apostles' Creed...*

*Our Father...*

**Faith**: For the grace to respond to Your call with childlike trust and gratitude.

*Hail Mary...*

**Hope**: For the grace to hope in Your plan for me and for the world.

*Hail Mary...*

**Love**: For the grace to love You above all and accept Your unconditional love for me.

*Hail Mary...*

*Glory be...*

*Fatima Prayer...*

The Joyful Mysteries open up to us the realization in time of the revelation of the salvation of God. Mary's assent to the will of God is the human *fiat* of the New Covenant... an act of trust undoing the failure of Eve. Jesus is conceived by the Holy Spirit and born of the Virgin Mary as the fulfillment of the protoevangelium of Genesis. He is the answer to the sorrows that have plagued humanity since our fall from grace. He comes to end our slavery to sin, lead us across the river of Baptism, and bring us home to paradise. He humbled Himself to be like us to raise us up to be like Him.

Spiritual Fruit: Faithfulness

## The First Joyful Mystery
# **Annunciation**

*"I will put enmity between you and the woman,/ and between your offspring and hers;/ They will strike at your head,/ while you strike at their heel"* (Gen 3:15). *"Behold, the virgin shall be with child and bear a son,/ and they shall name him Emmanuel,/"* which means *"God is with us."* (Matt 1:23). *...the angel Gabriel was sent... to a virgin betrothed to... Joseph, of the house of David, and the virgin's name was Mary. ..."Hail, favored one! The Lord is with you." ... Mary said, "Behold, I am the handmaid of the Lord. May it be done to me according to your word"* (Luke 1: 26-28, 38).

By his Revelation, *"the invisible God, from the fullness of his love, addresses men as his friends, and moves among them, in order to invite and receive them into his own company."* [DV 2; cf. Col 1:15; I Tim 1:17; Ex 33:11; Jn 15:14-15; Bar 3:38 (Vulg.)] *The adequate response to this invitation is faith* (CCC 142 [Cf. DV 5]). By faith, *man completely submits his intellect and his will to God. With his whole being man gives his assent to God the revealer. Sacred Scripture calls this human response to God, the author of revelation, "the obedience of faith"* (CCC 143 [Cf. Rom 1:5; 16:26]).

*Our Father…*

In disobedience, our first parents broke Covenant with God—He remains true to His promises. As Mary humbly accepted her role in salvation may I be obedient in all areas of my life.

*Hail Mary…*

Mary's relationship with Joseph was briefly complicated by her blessing. May I not abandon my blessings due to worldly considerations.

*Hail Mary…*

God wants the assent of free will, not robotic obedience. Lord, help me want to love You fully and without reservation.

*Hail Mary…*

*By… giving her consent to the Incarnation, Mary… is mother wherever he is Savior and head of the Mystical Body* (CCC 973). She was prepared from the moment of her conception to be the Ark of the New Covenant. My own station in life, with my gifts, has a purpose in God's plan.

*Hail Mary…*

*"The knot of Eve's disobedience was loosed by Mary's obedience"* (St Irenaeus). St Mary, Untier of Knots, free me from all that hinders me in following your example of faith.

*Hail Mary…*

As with Mary, God seeks an intimate relationship with me. May I not allow my sins to separate me from Him.

*Hail Mary…*

Mary's trust in God is absolute. She trusts that she will experience a miracle as reported by the angel. Do I truly believe in miracles? Do I believe a loving God is involved in the world today and He cares for me personally?

*Hail Mary…*

God sends messengers to me, too, in encounters of daily life. May I recognize the angels He sends—and may I also serve others.

*Hail Mary…*

In the Incarnation, the eternal Word took on temporal flesh. Lord, help me pray and work tirelessly to protect human life—from conception to natural death.

*Hail Mary...*

Mary conceived *the eternal Son of the Father in a humanity drawn from her own* (CCC 485). As You share in our humanity, help me aspire to holiness.

Hail Mary, full of grace.
The Lord is with thee.
Blessed art thou among women,
and blessed is the fruit of thy womb, Jesus.
Holy Mary, Mother of God, pray for us sinners,
now and at the hour of our death.
Amen.

Glory be to the Father,
to the Son, and
to the Holy Spirit,
as it was, is now, and
ever shall be, world without end.
Amen.

O my Jesus, forgive us our sins,
save us from the fires of Hell;
lead all souls to Heaven,
especially those who have
most need of your mercy.

Spiritual Fruit: Kindness

The Second Joyful Mystery
# Visitation

*"... How can the ark of the LORD come to me?" ... The ark of the LORD remained in the house of Obed-edom the Gittite for three months...* (2 Sam 6:9-11). *When Elizabeth heard Mary's greeting, the infant leaped in her womb, and Elizabeth, filled with the holy Spirit, cried out in a loud voice and said, "Most blessed are you among women, and blessed is the fruit of your womb. And how does this happen to me, that the mother of my Lord should come to me?" ... Mary remained with her about three months and then returned to her home.* (Luke 1:41-43, 56) *"Do to others whatever you would have them do to you. This is the law and the prophets"* (Matt 7:12).

The works of mercy *are charitable actions by which we come to the aid of our neighbor in his spiritual and bodily necessities* (CCC 2447 [Cf. Isa 58:6-7; Heb 13:3]). *When her mother reproached her for caring for the poor and the sick at home, St. Rose of Lima said to her: "When we serve the poor and the sick, we serve Jesus. We must not fail to help our neighbors, because in them we serve Jesus"* (CCC 2449 [P. Hansen, Vita mirabilis (Louvain, 1668)]).

*Our Father...*

When the Angel left her, Mary's next act was to go help her cousin Elizabeth. Mary, pray for me to follow your example of humble service to others.

*Hail Mary...*

You believed what the Angel told you about Elizabeth as evidenced in your action. May my belief animate my actions in service to the Kingdom.

*Hail Mary...*

We all sin and fall short of the glory of God (Rom 3:23). Others are not worse than me because they sin differently or more publicly than I do. I will be kind—always—and pray for reconciliation.

*Hail Mary...*

*"All generations will call me blessed"*: *"The Church's devotion to the Blessed Virgin is intrinsic to Christian worship"* (CCC 971 [Lk 1:48; Paul VI, MC 56]). Mary, I fly to your protection from the evil that infects the world.

*Hail Mary...*

Before he was born, John the Baptist, in the spirit of Elijah, leaped in the presence of his Lord. May I recognize that all are endowed with purpose from conception to natural death.

*Hail Mary...*

All of life is a gift from God. He gives and takes away according to His purpose. I will trust as I walk with Him and seek to love and serve Him in those made in His image and likeness.

*Hail Mary...*

Lord, help me recognize You in others.

*Hail Mary...*

Give me the grace to carry You to others.

*Hail Mary...*

The law of the Lord is love. In His love for us, God has given us our neighbors in need. *"The poor [we] will always have with [us]"* (Mark 14:7) because through service to them, we learn to love.

*Hail Mary...*

Mary's model of Christian service is doing household chores for Elizabeth. May I recognize that my Christian life often means doing small things with great love (St Teresa of Calcutta).

Hail Mary, full of grace.
The Lord is with thee.
Blessed art thou among women,
and blessed is the fruit of thy womb, Jesus.
Holy Mary, Mother of God, pray for us sinners,
now and at the hour of our death.
Amen.

Glory be to the Father,
to the Son, and
to the Holy Spirit,
as it was, is now, and
ever shall be, world without end.
Amen.

O my Jesus, forgive us our sins,
save us from the fires of Hell;
lead all souls to Heaven,
especially those who have
most need of your mercy.

Spiritual Fruit: Goodness

## The Third Joyful Mystery
# Nativity

*And the Word became flesh/ and made his dwelling among us...* (John 1:14). *For God so loved the world that he gave his only Son, so that everyone who believes in him might not perish but might have eternal life. For God did not send his Son into the world to condemn the world, but that the world might be saved through him* (John 3:16-17). *He is the image of the invisible God,/ the firstborn of all creation* (Col 1:15).

*To become a child in relation to God is the condition for entering the kingdom* [Cf. Mt 18:3-4]. *For this, we must humble ourselves and become little. ... Only when Christ is formed in us will the mystery of Christmas be fulfilled in us* (CCC 526 [Cf. Gal 4:19]).

*Our Father...*

Jesus, the King of all kings and God made flesh,
laid aside His glory to be born of a woman as a
helpless baby. How can I not be struck with awe
in contemplation of His humble majesty?

*Hail Mary...*

Mary bore a Son at Christmas who called me to
rebirth in Baptism—He became like me to make
me like Him. May I seek to imitate Christ in
thought, word, and deed.

*Hail Mary...*

The angels announced their tidings to shepherds. I
will remember that where man sees a shepherd,
God may see a king. I don't have to be "great" in
the eyes of the world to serve the Kingdom.

*Hail Mary...*

Lord, evil sought Your destruction at Your birth
and murdered the Holy Innocents. In following
You, I will face opposition from a world that
hates You. Help me not be discouraged.

*Hail Mary...*

Many want to encounter Christ on their own terms. Herod sought His life. Pilate questioned Him. Others sought miracles. May I approach Him in love, humility, gratitude, and supplication.

*Hail Mary...*

As a baby, Jesus laid quietly in the manger. St Joseph is often called "the Silent Saint." In my humble service to the Kingdom, may I not seek to glorify myself.

*Hail Mary...*

Heaven and Earth are full of God's glory. He is unchanging and constant. As a baptized child of God, may I help bring peace to troubled souls in a turbulent world.

*Hail Mary...*

Innkeepers had the opportunity to welcome God-in-the-flesh but denied Him a room. May I not fill my heart so full with the world that I leave no room for Him.

*Hail Mary...*

In answer to their need, God provided a stable
instead of an inn. He always answers… but not
always how we expect. He also says, "no." Lord,
I accept Your will in all ways—great and small.

*Hail Mary…*

The Wise Men brought gifts to God incarnate.
Do I give the best of the time, talents, and
treasure entrusted to me… or just what is left over
after sacrificing at the altars of the world?

Hail Mary, full of grace.
The Lord is with thee.
Blessed art thou among women,
and blessed is the fruit of thy womb, Jesus.
Holy Mary, Mother of God, pray for us sinners,
now and at the hour of our death.
Amen.

Glory be to the Father,
to the Son, and
to the Holy Spirit,
as it was, is now, and
ever shall be, world without end.
Amen.


O my Jesus, forgive us our sins,
save us from the fires of Hell;
lead all souls to Heaven,
especially those who have
most need of your mercy.

Spiritual Fruit: Patience

The Fourth Joyful Mystery
# Presentation

*... And the lord whom you seek will come suddenly to his temple... (Mal 3:1) ... they took him up to Jerusalem to present him to the Lord... and Simeon blessed them and said to Mary his mother, "Behold, this child is destined for the fall and rise of many in Israel, and to be a sign that will be contradicted (and you yourself a sword will pierce) so that the thoughts of many hearts may be revealed" (Luke 2:22, 34-35).*

*When the Church celebrates* the liturgy of Advent *each year, she makes present this ancient expectancy of the Messiah, for by sharing in the long preparation for the Savior's first coming, the faithful renew their ardent desire for his second coming* (CCC 524 [Cf Rev 22:17]).

*Our Father...*

Simeon was promised that he would see God's salvation before he died. He waited patiently for the day. May my soul be at peace in the assurance of our Lord's promises.

*Hail Mary...*

Approaching Christ is a decisive moment. In His intensity, am I clay or wax—will my heart harden or soften? I pray for all who are obstinate in sinfulness.

*Hail Mary...*

The sword of sorrow predicted for Mary anticipates her son's death on the cross (CCC 529). May I not run from my own cross but bear the trials of life with faith, humility, and patience.

*Hail Mary...*

The sword which pierces the heart of Mary lays bare the intentions of men—for and against her Son. As she tolerates the wanderings of my heart, may I bear the persecutions of the world.

*Hail Mary...*

Our Lord's religious life was that of a Jew obedient to the Law (CCC 531). He didn't place Himself above His people—He came to serve, not to be served. Lord, help me be obedient in my observance of obligation and devotion.

*Hail Mary...*

Joseph is a role model of strength, kindness, and devotion. He offers a poor man's substitute for a lamb. Help me offer sacrifices—even in small ways—for the glory of the Kingdom.

*Hail Mary...*

In reflection, I can see that many of my difficulties are the result of my own impatience. May I be at peace in the presence of my Lord and trust in His plan for me.

*Hail Mary...*

Simeon quickly recognized Christ and left satisfied with this one experience. Our Lord is present today in the Eucharist. I will spend time in adoration and receive Him frequently in Mass.

*Hail Mary...*

Christ is present in the "temple of the Holy Spirit"—my body (1 Cor 6:15-20). Lord, in Your love and mercy, help me respect what You have made holy.

*Hail Mary...*

As He prepared to leave, Jesus promised His return (Luke 21:27). May I have the patience of Simeon to live out my faith waiting in joyful hope for His coming in glory.

Hail Mary, full of grace.
The Lord is with thee.
Blessed art thou among women,
and blessed is the fruit of thy womb, Jesus.
Holy Mary, Mother of God, pray for us sinners,
now and at the hour of our death.
Amen.

Glory be to the Father,
to the Son, and
to the Holy Spirit,
as it was, is now, and
ever shall be, world without end.
Amen.


O my Jesus, forgive us our sins,
save us from the fires of Hell;
lead all souls to Heaven,
especially those who have
most need of your mercy.

Spiritual Fruit: Modesty

The Fifth Joyful Mystery
# Finding Jesus

*... "Do you understand what you are reading?" He replied, "How can I, unless someone instructs me?" (Acts 8:30-31) After three days they found him in the temple, sitting in the midst of the teachers, listening to them and asking them questions, and all who heard him were astounded at his understanding and his answers. ... He went down with them and came to Nazareth, and was obedient to them; and his mother kept all these things in her heart. (Luke 2:46-47, 51).*

*Here Jesus lets us catch a glimpse of the mystery of his total consecration to a mission that flows from his divine sonship: "Did you not know that I must be about my Father's work?" (CCC 534 [Lk 2:49 alt]) No one can believe alone, just as no one can live alone. You have not given yourself faith as you have not given yourself life. The believer has received faith from others and should hand it on to others. Our love for Jesus and for our neighbor impels us to speak to others about our faith. Each believer is thus a link in the great chain of believers (CCC 166).*

*Our Father...*

Lord, You were found "about [Your] Father's work." When You come again, may You find me also about Your Father's work.

*Hail Mary...*

There are dark times of the soul when I can't feel You near. I am comforted and grateful to know that You are still about Your Father's work in me.

*Hail Mary...*

Mary and Joseph searched for You. The longing in my soul can only be filled by You. May I seek, ask, and knock that I may find You, receive You, and come into Your presence.

*Hail Mary...*

When I feel distant from You, help me seek You in Your Word, at Mass, in Eucharistic Adoration, and by serving those made in Your image and likeness. Purify my heart so I may see Your face.

*Hail Mary...*

Jesus, though Son of God, was obedient to His earthly parents (CCC 532). He lived a normal life like ours (CCC 531). May my family resemble the Holy Family in love and fidelity to God's plan.

*Hail Mary…*

Through Baptism I am also a child of God. Help me imitate Your devotion to our Father's will. In moments of weakness, I will turn to You in prayer to be led and strengthened by You.

*Hail Mary…*

The Temple was the model of Heaven on Earth. Jesus was at home. May I recognize the reality of Heaven in Mass as I worship in the company of saints and angels.

*Hail Mary…*

"Why have You done this to us?" Mary's question to Jesus is a mother's reproach for her distress. Lord, grant me the grace to express myself openly and honestly in my prayers to You.

*Hail Mary…*

Joseph and Mary "did not understand" Your answer, and yet they accepted it in faith (CCC 534). May I have the grace to accept Your answers to my prayers—especially when I least understand.

*Hail Mary…*

Jesus amazed His audience in the Temple with His understanding and answers. Like Mary, may I prayerfully contemplate these things in my heart and pass on the faith like sharing a candle flame.

Hail Mary, full of grace.
The Lord is with thee.
Blessed art thou among women,
and blessed is the fruit of thy womb, Jesus.
Holy Mary, Mother of God, pray for us sinners,
now and at the hour of our death.
Amen.

*Glory be…*

*Fatima Prayer…*

# The
# Luminous Mysteries

*Apostles' Creed...*

*Our Father...*

**Faith**: May I see in myself a reflection of the Lord and live my life in faithful imitation of Him.

*Hail Mary...*

**Hope**: For the hope that animates the Church in preparation for Christ's return.

*Hail Mary...*

**Love**: For opportunities to show unconditional love to the Lord and to all who are made in His image and likeness.

*Hail Mary...*

*Glory be...*

*Fatima Prayer...*

The Luminous Mysteries remind us who Christ is. They illuminate His identity... and our own in communion with Him. He is Son of God, Son of Man (Mary), King, Prophet, and Priest. We enter into these mysteries by recognizing we are the Body of Christ through Baptism and creation in the image and likeness of God. We are called to obedience and evangelization, bringing the good news of salvation—being priests in the domestic churches of our homes and communities. We are His hands and feet carrying on the Great Commission to the ends of the Earth.

Revelation: Son of God

The First Luminous Mystery
# Baptism

*After all the people had been baptized and Jesus also had been baptized and was praying, heaven was opened and the holy Spirit descended upon him in bodily form like a dove. And a voice came from heaven, "You are my beloved Son; with you I am well pleased" (Luke 3:21-22). For you did not receive a spirit of slavery to fall back into fear, but you received a spirit of adoption, through which we cry, "Abba, Father!" The Spirit itself bears witness with our spirit that we are children of God, and if children, then heirs, heirs of God and joint heirs with Christ, if only we suffer with him so that we may also be glorified with him (Rom 8:15-17).*

*The Word became flesh to make us* "partakers of the divine nature" [2 Pt 1:4]: *"For this is why the Word became man, and the Son of God became the Son of man: so that man, by entering into communion with the Word and thus receiving divine sonship, might become a son of God"* (CCC 460 [St. Irenaeus, Adv. haeres. 3, 19, 1: PG 7/1, 939]).

*Our Father...*

Light from light and true God from true God,
Jesus is the light of truth. May I not hide the light
given in Baptism but help dispel the darkness
in our fallen world.

*Hail Mary...*

Lord, You are not ashamed to call sinners
"brothers." You raised me in Baptism to new life as
a child of God in Your holy family. This life comes
with the cross. Give me courage to follow You.

*Hail Mary...*

The waters of Baptism are sanctified by Your
presence. You entered with me and washed me
clean of spiritual afflictions. May I guard my soul
from the stain of sin and share my joy with others.

*Hail Mary...*

In your great love for me, help me love You with
my whole heart, soul, mind, and strength... and
love all who are made in Your image and
likeness as I love myself.

*Hail Mary...*

You did not consider equality with God something to be grasped, but making Yourself one of us, You humbled Yourself. May I be humble in communion with You.

*Hail Mary...*

Lamb of God, I am not worthy to loosen Your sandal straps. You take away my sins and invite me home to heavenly glory. May my spirit be at peace and rejoice in Your mercy.

*Hail Mary...*

Through Baptism, You have made me a member of Your holy household and a partaker in Your divine nature (Eph 1:5). May I not scandalize those who would see You through me.

*Hail Mary...*

Through Baptism, You have made me a temple of the Holy Spirit (1 Cor 3:16). I reject the devil, all of his works, and all of his empty promises. May Your Spirit animate my every thought, word, and deed.

*Hail Mary...*

As a baptized child of the holy household of
Heaven, may I please our heavenly Father in the
example of Christ who faithfully fulfills the
purpose for which He is sent (Is 55:11).

*Hail Mary...*

God the Father is our example of perfect
fatherhood, God the Son of perfect sonship, and
God the Holy Spirit of unity in love. May I live
my own vocation in diligent fidelity to His will.

Hail Mary, full of grace.
The Lord is with thee.
Blessed art thou among women,
and blessed is the fruit of thy womb, Jesus.
Holy Mary, Mother of God, pray for us sinners,
now and at the hour of our death.
Amen.

Glory be to the Father,
to the Son, and
to the Holy Spirit,
as it was, is now, and
ever shall be, world without end.
Amen.


O my Jesus, forgive us our sins,
save us from the fires of Hell;
lead all souls to Heaven,
especially those who have
most need of your mercy.

Revelation: Son of Man

The Second Luminous Mystery
# Wedding at Cana

*But his servants came up and reasoned with him: "My father, if the prophet told you to do something extraordinary, would you not do it? All the more since he told you, 'Wash, and be clean'?" (2 Kings 5:13). When the wine ran short, the mother of Jesus said to him, "They have no wine."... His mother said to the servers, "Do whatever he tells you." ... Jesus told them, "Fill the jars with water." So they filled them to the brim (John 2:3-7). He will change our lowly body to conform with his glorified body by the power that enables him also to bring all things into subjection to himself (Phil 3:21).*

*The Church attaches great importance to Jesus' presence at the wedding at Cana. She sees in it the confirmation of the goodness of marriage and the proclamation that thenceforth marriage will be an efficacious sign of Christ's presence (CCC 1613). The Christian home is the place where children receive the first proclamation of the faith. For this reason the family home is rightly called "the domestic church," a community of grace and prayer, a school of human virtues and of Christian charity (CCC 1666).*

*Our Father…*

Mary brings to Jesus the trouble she sees but
doesn't tell Him what to do. Rather, she turns to
me and says, "do whatever He tells you."
Let this be my walk of faith.

*Hail Mary…*

In my prayers, I will bring to Jesus my troubles
without demanding my own solutions. Like
Naaman the Syrian's lesson, my trust should be
deep enough to accept His answers.

*Hail Mary…*

Mary is the vessel bringing Christ to the world.
May I be a vessel today in the Church—bringing
Christ to a community in need. May I die to myself
in sacrificial giving as Christ died for His Bride.

*Hail Mary…*

At Cana, Jesus does not act without being asked. I
will pray from the deepest desires of my heart for
Him to fulfill my needs in His own way and time.

*Hail Mary…*

When water became wine, Christ changed something common into something refined. May the unseen change in me from Baptism be revealed in my love for Him and others.

*Hail Mary...*

His *disciples began to believe in him* with this miracle (John 2:11). Lord, thank You for the grace to witness the greater miracle at each Mass.

*Hail Mary...*

The stewards sought a solution to their problem. Mary told them to obey You. Studying Your word and knowing Your commandments aren't enough... I must do what I learn (James 1:22).

*Hail Mary...*

If I bring my needs to Mary, she will turn to her Son in supplication. May my inward gaze contemplate the majesty of our Lord and trust Him. His grace is sufficient.

*Hail Mary...*

In the desert, Christ resisted the temptation to perform miracles for His own benefit (Matt 4:1-11)—then acquiesced to a simple request to help others in Cana. My blessings aren't just for my own enjoyment—they are meant to be shared.

*Hail Mary…*

The family is the reflection of the Trinity and under greatest attack from the enemy who hates You (CCC 239). I will respect the image of the family given to us by Scripture and the Church.

Hail Mary, full of grace.
The Lord is with thee.
Blessed art thou among women,
and blessed is the fruit of thy womb, Jesus.
Holy Mary, Mother of God, pray for us sinners,
now and at the hour of our death.
Amen.

Glory be to the Father,
to the Son, and
to the Holy Spirit,
as it was, is now, and
ever shall be, world without end.
Amen.


O my Jesus, forgive us our sins,
save us from the fires of Hell;
lead all souls to Heaven,
especially those who have
most need of your mercy.

Revelation: King

The Third Luminous Mystery
# Proclaiming the Kingdom

*... I saw coming with the clouds of heaven/ One like a son of man./ ... He received dominion, splendor, and kingship;/ all nations, peoples and tongues will serve him./ His dominion is an everlasting dominion/ that shall not pass away...* (Dan 7:13-14). *From that time on, Jesus began to preach and say, "Repent, for the kingdom of heaven is at hand"* (Matt 4:17). *... "Amen, I say to you, unless you turn and become like children, you will not enter the kingdom of heaven. Whoever humbles himself like this child is the greatest in the kingdom of heaven"* (Matt 18:3-4).

*By his word, through signs that manifest the reign of God, and by sending out his disciples, Jesus calls all people to come together around him. But above all in the great Paschal mystery —his death on the cross and his Resurrection— he would accomplish the coming of his kingdom. "And I, when I am lifted up from the earth, will draw all men to myself." Into this union with Christ all men are called* (CCC 542 [Jn 12:32; cf. LG 3]).

*Our Father...*

*"The kingdom of heaven was inaugurated on earth by Christ. ... The Church is the seed and beginning of this kingdom"* (CCC 567). I will trust what Christ is building.

*Hail Mary...*

Lord, You are the Good Shepherd who came to gather Your lost sheep. Thank You for Your mercy to me... a sinner.

*Hail Mary...*

The Gospel is the seed sown in the world. Help me nurture the seed in my soul so that it won't be choked by a world of distractions.

*Hail Mary...*

Your Kingdom is the greatest treasure and the goal of all longing. Help me let go of all that keeps me from accepting what You offer.

*Hail Mary...*

You set Your Apostles as ministers of the Kingdom and gave them real authority in Heaven and Earth. They bind and loose (Matt 16:19). I will respect apostolic authority and pray for it to be wisely exercised.

*Hail Mary…*

Help me not seek exaltation in this life that I may focus on my inheritance in Your eternal Kingdom. May I be childlike in my relationship with You… dependent and grateful.

*Hail Mary…*

I believe in the Apostolic Succession yet I have brothers in the Kingdom not in communion with the Church. You prayed for all to be one in faith. I will not encourage division among Your followers (Mark 9:38-41 & Luke 11:23 & John 10:16).

*Hail Mary…*

You are the vine. I am a branch grafted in Baptism. Apart from You, I can do nothing. May my life bear fruit investing the time, talent, and treasure entrusted to me into growing Your Kingdom.

*Hail Mary…*

The Kingdom of Heaven is not in the carnal pleasures of this world. In the proper ordering of my passions, may I find fulfillment in charity and divine beatitude (CCC 1769).

*Hail Mary...*

*Everyone is called to enter the Kingdom* (CCC 543). The Kingdom is here and now where God's will is done. May I live to serve now and patiently await the everlasting joy to come.

Hail Mary, full of grace.
The Lord is with thee.
Blessed art thou among women,
and blessed is the fruit of thy womb, Jesus.
Holy Mary, Mother of God, pray for us sinners,
now and at the hour of our death.
Amen.

Glory be to the Father,
to the Son, and
to the Holy Spirit,
as it was, is now, and
ever shall be, world without end.
Amen.


O my Jesus, forgive us our sins,
save us from the fires of Hell;
lead all souls to Heaven,
especially those who have
most need of your mercy.

Revelation: Prophet

## The Fourth Luminous Mystery
# Transfiguration

*A prophet like me will the LORD, your God, raise up for you from among your own kindred; that is the one to whom you shall listen (Deut 18:15). And he was transfigured before them; his face shone like the sun and his clothes became white as light. And behold, Moses and Elijah appeared to them... then from the cloud came a voice that said, "This is my beloved Son, with whom I am well pleased; listen to him" (Matt 17:2-3, 5).*

*The Transfiguration gives us a foretaste of Christ's glorious coming, when he "will change our lowly body to be like his glorious body" [Phil 3:21]. But it also recalls that "it is through many persecutions that we must enter the kingdom of God" (CCC 556 [Acts 14:22]).*

*Our Father…*

Lord, in Your radiance we find the hope of the
Resurrection. Give me the courage to follow You
to the cross that I may rise with You
to heavenly glory.

*Hail Mary…*

You radiated heavenly glory yet spoke of Your
coming Passion. The cross is Your love revealed,
not an obstacle in Your path. Help me
sacrificially live my love for You.

*Hail Mary…*

You climbed the mountain to pray. Help me find
times of quiet reflection to more readily
enter Your mysteries.

*Hail Mary…*

Christ is seen with Moses and Elijah, representing
the Law and the Prophets. Lord, You stand at the
center of all history—before and since. As You
speak, may I have the grace to listen.

*Hail Mary…*

Moses was given the Law. Elijah proclaimed
Your words. You are the Word Incarnate. Help
me be diligent in the study of Scripture…
the study of You… and follow where You lead.

*Hail Mary…*

You were transfigured in prayer. Help me enter
into communion with You as I pray and
contemplate the light of truth.

*Hail Mary…*

The Apostles saw Christ as He truly is. I can see
His image and likeness in the people I meet.
May I see and love Him in them… not
focus on their faults.

*Hail Mary…*

In the cloud of God's presence, the Father
confirms Peter's proclamation—Jesus is the Son
of God. May I be still in the realization of Your
majesty. Jesus, I trust in You.

*Hail Mary…*

The light came into the world but men preferred darkness (John 3:19)—while we can't put out the Sun, we can close the blinds. In my hunger and thirst for righteousness, help me seek Your transfigured glory and worship You.

*Hail Mary...*

Even the miraculous may seem commonplace when it becomes routine. May the glory of Your love revealed on the cross continually renew my passion and give me courage to follow You to crucified glory.

Hail Mary, full of grace.
The Lord is with thee.
Blessed art thou among women,
and blessed is the fruit of thy womb, Jesus.
Holy Mary, Mother of God, pray for us sinners,
now and at the hour of our death.
Amen.

Glory be to the Father,
to the Son, and
to the Holy Spirit,
as it was, is now, and
ever shall be, world without end.
Amen.


O my Jesus, forgive us our sins,
save us from the fires of Hell;
lead all souls to Heaven,
especially those who have
most need of your mercy.

Revelation: Priest

The Fifth Luminous Mystery
# Eucharist

*"... unless you eat the flesh of the Son of Man and drink his blood, you do not have life within you. Whoever eats my flesh and drinks my blood has eternal life, and I will raise him on the last day. For my flesh is true food, and my blood is true drink. Whoever eats my flesh and drinks my blood remains in me and I in him"*(John 6:53-56)....*Jesus took bread... and giving it to his disciples said, "Take and eat; this is my body... this is my blood of the covenant..."* (Matt 26:26-28). *The cup of blessing that we bless, is it not a participation in the blood of Christ? The bread that we break, is it not a participation in the body of Christ?* (1 Cor 10:16).

*There is no surer pledge or dearer sign of this great hope in the new heavens and new earth "in which righteousness dwells,"* [2 Pet 3:13] *than the Eucharist. Every time this mystery is celebrated, "the work of our redemption is carried on" and we "break the one bread that provides the medicine of immortality, the antidote for death, and the food that makes us live forever in Jesus Christ"* (CCC 1405 [LG 3; St. Ignatius of Antioch, Ad Eph. 20, 2: SCh 10, 76]).

*Our Father...*

The same voice that spoke creation into being now declares bread and wine His body and blood. In each repeated consecration, we share in the first (CCC 1410). May my respect for this universal communion of love be reflected in my demeanor.

*Hail Mary...*

Receiving *in faith the gift of his Eucharist is to receive the Lord himself* (CCC 1336). Lord, may I satisfy my soul's hunger and thirst for You with You alone in the Mass You instituted.

*Hail Mary...*

In the Eucharist, we are united with You. *Christ enables us to live in him all that he himself lived, and he lives it in us* (CCC 521). You are priest forever and Your flesh offered for me sustains me on my journey home (CCC 1392).

*Hail Mary...*

In the Eucharist, we offer to the Father what He Himself has given us (CCC 1368). It is truly right and just, my duty and salvation—always and everywhere—to give Him thanks.

*Hail Mary...*

*Jesus includes the apostles in his own offering and bids them perpetuate it… as priests…* (CCC 611 [Cf. Lk 22:19]). Lord, help me recognize my own priestly mission in offering You to others.

*Hail Mary…*

Soon after their priestly calling, Judas betrayed You and almost all of the others deserted You. May I not despair of my failings but be continually reconciled with You and Your Bride, the Church.

*Hail Mary…*

The hemorrhaging woman was healed by her faith in touching Your clothes. I receive You— body, blood, soul, and divinity—at each Mass. May I never doubt Your healing power.

*Hail Mary…*

Lord, Your presence in the Sacrament doesn't depend on my belief (CCC 1377). Approaching communion is approaching You. I will respect what I receive in sincere reverence and humility.

*Hail Mary…*

I come to the Eucharist not because I am worthy.
I am a sinner. My Lord who calls me is worthy.
Lord, help me prepare myself to participate fully
in the mystery (CCC 1385).

*Hail Mary...*

The Eucharist is our unique physical encounter
with Christ on Earth. It is the sum and summary
of our faith (CCC 1327)—the Marriage Feast of
Christ and His Bride, the Church. Heaven and
Earth are united in worship (CCC 1370). Blessed
are those called to the Supper of the Lamb!

Hail Mary, full of grace.
The Lord is with thee.
Blessed art thou among women,
and blessed is the fruit of thy womb, Jesus.
Holy Mary, Mother of God, pray for us sinners,
now and at the hour of our death.
Amen.

*Glory be...*

*Fatima Prayer...*

# The
# Sorrowful Mysteries

*Apostles' Creed...*

*Our Father...*

**Faith**: For the grace to trust God's holy will in the midst of trials.

*Hail Mary...*

**Hope**: Lord, You are the light of hope in the midst of darkness.

*Hail Mary...*

**Love**: For the grace to love those hardest to love in the midst of persecution.

*Hail Mary...*

*Glory be...*

*Fatima Prayer...*

The Sorrowful Mysteries are the greatest love story ever told. No man has greater love than to die for his friends (John 15:13)... how much greater the love when dying for his torturers! What is love if not self-denial for someone else? What is self-denial without sacrifice? Christ was crucified, died, and was buried for us while we were yet sinners. He suffered a death we deserve. Sinless Himself, He took on our shame and bore it in His flesh. We are called to take up our crosses and follow His example of sacrificial love.

Virtue: Prudence

The First Sorrowful Mystery
# Agony in the Garden

*But it was the LORD's will to crush him with pain./ By making his life as a reparation offering/ ... the LORD's will shall be accomplished through him./Because of his anguish he shall see the light;/ because of his knowledge he shall be content;/ My servant, the just one, shall justify the many,/ their iniquity he shall bear (Is 53:10-11). Then he said to them, "My soul is sorrowful even to death. Remain here and keep watch with me." He advanced a little and fell prostrate in prayer, saying, "My Father, if it is possible, let this cup pass from me; yet, not as I will, but as you will." When he returned to his disciples he found them asleep (Matt 26:38-40).*

*It is not easy for man, wounded by sin, to maintain moral balance. Christ's gift of salvation offers us the grace necessary to persevere in the pursuit of the virtues (CCC 1811). Such a battle and such a victory become possible only through prayer. It is by his prayer that Jesus vanquishes the Tempter, both at the outset of his public mission and in the ultimate struggle of his agony (CCC 2849 [Cf. Mt 4:1-11; 26:36-44]).*

*Our Father...*

Lord, You knew what the next day brought for You because of my sins. Thank You for accepting the cup that bought my salvation.

*Hail Mary...*

I am grateful that You would have suffered and died for me even if I were the only sinner. I keep Your passion close to my heart—especially on Fridays— with penitential offerings.

*Hail Mary...*

Whether You dreaded Your passion or groaned to complete Your mission (St Catherine of Siena), You prayed that Your Father's will be done, not Your own. Help me pray as You do.

*Hail Mary...*

You prayed alone. Help me keep watch with You in my heart and unite my prayers to Yours. May my faith not be lukewarm nor indifferent to Your sacrificial love for me.

*Hail Mary...*

When Your prayers were done, You were met by Your betrayer. You do not delight in the death of the wicked (Ez 18:23). Help me forgive and not hold guilty those who betray me.

*Hail Mary...*

You had power and authority to shape Your own life according to Your own will. You did the will of Your Father. Help me be humble and faithful in the exercise of my own responsibilities.

*Hail Mary...*

Peter slept in the Garden, distanced himself at Your arrest, and denied knowing You. May I not be so proud as to think I could do better when tested. Thank you for Your grace and mercy to me, a sinner.

*Hail Mary...*

Lord, You were arrested on false charges and denied mercy. Help me forgive and be merciful when I am persecuted.

*Hail Mary...*

You asked the sleeping disciples to keep watch with You. They disobeyed and gave in to their desire for material comfort. That's often the reason I sin. Forgive me.

*Hail Mary…*

Lord, help me see in my own sufferings what I see in Yours… God working a greater good.

Hail Mary, full of grace.
The Lord is with thee.
Blessed art thou among women,
and blessed is the fruit of thy womb, Jesus.
Holy Mary, Mother of God, pray for us sinners,
now and at the hour of our death.
Amen.

Glory be to the Father,
to the Son, and
to the Holy Spirit,
as it was, is now, and
ever shall be, world without end.
Amen.


O my Jesus, forgive us our sins,
save us from the fires of Hell;
lead all souls to Heaven,
especially those who have
most need of your mercy.

Virtue: Justice

The Second Sorrowful Mystery
# Scourging at the Pillar

*Yet it was our pain that he bore,/ our sufferings he endured./ We thought of him as stricken,/ struck down by God and afflicted,/ But he was pierced for our sins,/ crushed for our iniquity./ He bore the punishment that makes us whole,/ by his wounds we were healed* (Is 53:4-5). *So Pilate, wishing to satisfy the crowd, released Barabbas to them and, after he had Jesus scourged, handed him over to be crucified* (Mark 15:15).

*Man, tempted by the devil, let his trust in his Creator die in his heart and, abusing his freedom, disobeyed God's command. This is what man's first sin consisted of* [Cf. Gen 3:1-11 ; Rom 5:19]. *All subsequent sin would be disobedience toward God and lack of trust in his goodness* (CCC 397). *Taking into account the fact that our sins affect Christ himself* [Cf. Mt 25:45; Acts 9:4-5], *the Church does not hesitate to impute to Christians the gravest responsibility for the torments inflicted upon Jesus...* (CCC 598).

*Our Father...*

Lord, You accepted the punishment for my sins (2 Cor 5:21). Help me see Your stripes in the hour of temptation and recoil at the image of Your suffering.

*Hail Mary...*

With each strike of the whip (flagrum), I can imagine the accusing voice of the devil announcing my sins which cause Your suffering. I pray for the grace to turn from sin and avoid temptation.

*Hail Mary...*

When I am tempted to unnaturally fulfill the desires of my flesh, may I envision Your pain and deny temptation through conscious acts of self-denial.

*Hail Mary...*

When I am tempted to take what is not meant for me, may I envision Your stripes and deny temptation through acts of charity.

*Hail Mary...*

When I am tempted to pridefully make of myself more than God has made me to be, may I envision Your sorrow and humble myself in prayer.

*Hail Mary...*

Lord, as You suffered to atone for my sins and Your mother suffered with You in her love for You, may I have the grace to offer my suffering and sacrifices for others.

*Hail Mary...*

Tortured unjustly, You uttered no cry. Help me be patient in the midst of suffering.

*Hail Mary...*

Help me not be jealous of the blessings of others but instead pray for all to realize the joy of salvation—especially those who persecute me.

*Hail Mary...*

Sins are not mistakes. I pray for forgiveness for my transgressions against You as, though angry, I forgive those who intentionally hurt me.

*Hail Mary...*

My Lord, I am sorry for my sins which offend You and deserve God's just punishments. You are all good and deserving of my love. I firmly resolve, with Your grace, to avoid temptations to sin.

Hail Mary, full of grace.
The Lord is with thee.
Blessed art thou among women,
and blessed is the fruit of thy womb, Jesus.
Holy Mary, Mother of God, pray for us sinners,
now and at the hour of our death.
Amen.


Glory be to the Father,
to the Son, and
to the Holy Spirit,
as it was, is now, and
ever shall be, world without end.
Amen.

O my Jesus, forgive us our sins,
save us from the fires of Hell;
lead all souls to Heaven,
especially those who have
most need of your mercy.

Virtue: Temperance

The Third Sorrowful Mystery
# Crowning with Thorns

*I gave my back to those who beat me,/ my cheeks to those who tore out my beard;/ My face I did not hide/ from insults and spitting.// The Lord God is my help,/ therefore I am not disgraced;/ Therefore I have set my face like flint,/ knowing that I shall not be put to shame* (Is 50:6-7). *They clothed him in purple and, weaving a crown of thorns, placed it on him. They began to salute him with "Hail, King of the Jews!" and kept striking his head with a reed and spitting upon him. They knelt before him in homage. And when they had mocked him, they stripped him of the purple cloak, dressed him in his own clothes, and led him out to crucify him* (Mark 15:17-20). *In fact, all who want to live religiously in Christ Jesus will be persecuted* (2 Tim 3:12).

*On the cross Christ took upon himself the whole weight of evil and took away the "sin of the world," [Jn 1:29; cf. Isa 53:4-6] ... By his passion and death on the cross Christ has given a new meaning to suffering: it can henceforth configure us to him and unite us with his redemptive Passion* (CCC 1505).

*Our Father...*

Lord, You are the King of all kings… yet You humbly removed Your crown to accept one of thorns. Your suffering is a crown of love. Help me love sacrificially in communion with You.

*Hail Mary...*

You came in the name of the Father and were mocked as a prophet. Help me not shrink from my own duty in the face of ridicule.

*Hail Mary...*

You were rejected by men. May I not seek the approval of men who reject You. I will remember that I most resemble You, the Man of Sorrows, in suffering for the Kingdom.

*Hail Mary...*

The world will hate me most when I most resemble You. You were cruelly beaten. May I have the grace to turn my other cheek when attacked and may my suffering be salvific for those I love.

*Hail Mary...*

The soldiers felt greater than You in the power they had been given over You. Help me remember the poor and helpless in my most exalted moments.

*Hail Mary…*

When You fed the multitudes, they sought to make You a king (John 6:15). You would only accept a crown of thorns. May my love for You be revealed in my humility and love for others.

*Hail Mary…*

Lord, the thorns which pierced You prick the conscience of all who sin (Abp Fulton J. Sheen). Help me turn from wicked thoughts and desires to humble prayer and self-denial.

*Hail Mary…*

May I not wear a crown of indignation for my own minor hardships but rather be humble and contrite in realization of my own sinfulness.

*Hail Mary…*

In frequent confessions to You, help me cut
deeply to rend my soul in trust and humility.
May my vulnerability to You be modeled after
Your own humility before the world's contempt.

*Hail Mary...*

I will rejoice when I am persecuted for the name of
Jesus. By meditating on the mysteries of the
Rosary, may I imitate what is contained and be
more fully conformed to Him who
suffered and died for me.

Hail Mary, full of grace.
The Lord is with thee.
Blessed art thou among women,
and blessed is the fruit of thy womb, Jesus.
Holy Mary, Mother of God, pray for us sinners,
now and at the hour of our death.
Amen.

Glory be to the Father,
to the Son, and
to the Holy Spirit,
as it was, is now, and
ever shall be, world without end.
Amen.

O my Jesus, forgive us our sins,
save us from the fires of Hell;
lead all souls to Heaven,
especially those who have
most need of your mercy.

Virtue: Fortitude

The Fourth Sorrowful Mystery
# Carrying the Cross

*Though harshly treated, he submitted/ and did not open his mouth;/ Like a lamb led to slaughter/ or a sheep silent before shearers,/ he did not open his mouth./ Seized and condemned, he was taken away./ Who would have thought any more of his destiny* (Is 53:7-8)? *... and carrying the cross himself he went out to what is called the Place of the Skull, in Hebrew, Golgotha* (John 19:17). *... they took hold of a certain Simon... and after laying the cross on him, they made him carry it behind Jesus* (Luke 23:26).

*The cross is the unique sacrifice of Christ, the "one mediator between God and men"* [1 Tim 2:5]. *But because in his incarnate divine person he has in some way united himself to every man, "the possibility of being made partners, in a way known to God, in the paschal mystery" is offered to all men* [GS 22 # 5; cf. # 2]. *He calls his disciples to "take up [their] cross and follow [him]"* [Mt 16:24], *for "Christ also suffered for [us], leaving [us] an example so that [we] should follow in his steps"* (CCC 618 [I Pt 2:21]).

*Our Father...*

The cross laid on Christ wasn't just made of wood... He bore the weight of our sins. He carried it for the guilty. He carried it for me.

*Hail Mary...*

Lord, You called us to take up our crosses daily and follow You. Help me be diligent in carrying my cross until the day You call me home.

*Hail Mary...*

The cross You carried was not of Your making. May I not rebel at carrying the cross I have helped fashion for myself.

*Hail Mary...*

You became a spectacle in Your infirmity. May I be willing to be thought a fool for the wisdom of God.

*Hail Mary...*

While suffering, You still thought of others—the women and children and Your tormentors. Grant me the grace to comfort and offer up my sufferings for others.

*Hail Mary...*

You fell. When I fall under the weight of my own cross, help me rise again in the hope I have in You.

*Hail Mary…*

May I not desire someone else's cross—which seems light to me—but accept that all carry crosses… and most are heavier than my own. Help me help others with their crosses.

*Hail Mary…*

The cross I carry is framed by self-denial. Though I try to have my own way, God created me with His own purpose in mind. Let my path of conversion be my ongoing assent to the will of God.

*Hail Mary…*

Abandoned by friends and rejected by the crowd, You were alone. Thank You for the assurance that I do not carry my cross alone. You have not given me a spirit of fear. I trust You in the darkest moments.

*Hail Mary…*

From a lowly manger-crib to the rejection of
Your people, Your whole life was lived under the
sign of persecution—and we share it with You
(CCC 530). In following You, I recognize that
my walk of faith is my lifelong way of the cross.

Hail Mary, full of grace.
The Lord is with thee.
Blessed art thou among women,
and blessed is the fruit of thy womb, Jesus.
Holy Mary, Mother of God, pray for us sinners,
now and at the hour of our death.
Amen.

Glory be to the Father,
to the Son, and
to the Holy Spirit,
as it was, is now, and
ever shall be, world without end.
Amen.

O my Jesus, forgive us our sins,
save us from the fires of Hell;
lead all souls to Heaven,
especially those who have
most need of your mercy.

Virtue: Charity

The Fifth Sorrowful Mystery
# Crucifixion

*My God, my God, why have You abandoned me? ...
They have pierced my hands and my feet/ I can
count all my bones./ They stare at me and gloat;/
they divide my garments among them;/ for my
clothing they cast lots. ...[God] has not spurned
or disdained/ the misery of this poor wretch,/ Did
not turn away from me,/ but heard me when I
cried out. (Ps 22:2, 17-19, 25). After this ... in
order that the scripture might be fulfilled, Jesus
said, "I thirst." ... When Jesus had taken the
wine, he said, "It is finished." And bowing his
head, he handed over the spirit (John 19:28-30).*

*The desire to embrace his Father's plan of
redeeming love inspired Jesus' whole life [Cf Lk
12:50; 22:15; Mt 16:21-23], for his redemptive
passion was the very reason for his Incarnation
(CCC 607). In fact, Jesus desires to associate with
his redeeming sacrifice those who were to be its
first beneficiaries [Cf Mk 10:39; Jn 21:18-19; Col
1:24].... "Apart from the cross there is no other
ladder by which we may get to heaven" (CCC
618 [St. Rose of Lima: cf. P. Hansen, Vita
mirabilis (Louvain, 1668)]).*

*Our Father…*

Lord, You went to the cross out of love for me.
Help me hold nothing back from You out of
love for You (Rom 12:1). My life is Yours.

*Hail Mary…*

You were faithful to fulfill all things on the cross.
Help me not shrink from my own duty
when it becomes difficult.

*Hail Mary…*

You forgave those who took Your life. Help me
forgive and pray for my enemies when it is hardest.

*Hail Mary…*

You took pity on the crowd and taught them
through the Psalm. Help me preach the Gospel
with my life… and use words when necessary.

*Hail Mary…*

As Your mother grieved, You acknowledged her
to Your Apostle and, by extension, Your Church.
May I stand with her at the foot of the cross
contemplating the destruction wrought by sin.

*Hail Mary…*

Help me see Your love in the sign of the cross and may I not run from love when confronting my own cross.

*Hail Mary...*

Jesus had hundreds of disciples but only twelve Apostles. Only three Apostles accompanied Him further into the Garden. Only one stood at the foot of the cross. The crowd thins as we approach the cross. I pray for the grace to stand with You—even if I stand alone.

*Hail Mary...*

Without Good Friday, there would be no Easter (Fr John Corapi). When evil surrounds me, I pray in joyful hope for the coming of Your Kingdom.

*Hail Mary...*

On the cross, You welcomed the thief in his contrition. In dying, You destroyed our death. May I never despair of Your mercy.

*Hail Mary...*

Without Christ, the cross is only wood. As You sanctified an instrument of torture into an image of love, sanctify me to live sacrificially as a reflection of Your love.

Hail Mary, full of grace.
The Lord is with thee.
Blessed art thou among women,
and blessed is the fruit of thy womb, Jesus.
Holy Mary, Mother of God, pray for us sinners,
now and at the hour of our death. Amen.

Glory be to the Father,
to the Son, and
to the Holy Spirit,
as it was, is now, and
ever shall be, world without end. Amen.

O my Jesus, forgive us our sins,
save us from the fires of Hell;
lead all souls to Heaven,
especially those who have
most need of your mercy.

# The
# Glorious Mysteries

*Apostles' Creed...*

*Our Father...*

**Faith**: For the grace to joyfully look beyond this world to my heavenly home.

*Hail Mary...*

**Hope**: For the grace to hope as I walk in this valley of tears.

*Hail Mary...*

**Love**: For the grace to love the eternal things of Heaven over the fading things of Earth.

*Hail Mary...*

*Glory be...*

*Fatima Prayer...*

In the Glorious Mysteries, our attention is on the resurrection of the body and the life of the world to come. Christ came to call all people to Himself. He restored in His perfect obedience what was lost in our first parents' disobedience: our inheritance as children of God. In His death, He promised life. In His resurrection is the promise of life everlasting. He rose from the dead, ascended into Heaven, and is seated at the right hand of God where He has gone to prepare a place for us. Mary's Assumption and Coronation presage our eternal reward in Heaven. By following her example of faithful obedience here, we hope to follow her to glory there.

Spiritual Fruit: Joy

The First Glorious Mystery
# Resurrection

*For you will not abandon my soul to Sheol,/ nor let your devout one see the pit (Psalm 16:10). ... he showed them his hands and his side. The disciples then rejoiced when they saw the Lord (John 20:20). For if we have grown into union with him through a death like his, we shall also be united with him in the resurrection. We know that our old self was crucified with him... that we might no longer be in slavery to sin (Romans 6:5-6). Blessed be the God and Father of our Lord Jesus Christ, who in his great mercy gave us a new birth to a living hope through the resurrection of Jesus Christ from the dead... (1 Peter 1:3). If then you were raised with Christ, seek what is above, where Christ is seated at the right hand of God (Col 3:1).*

*Baptism, the original and full sign of which is immersion, efficaciously signifies the descent into the tomb by the Christian who dies to sin with Christ in order to live a new life. "We were buried therefore with him by baptism into death, so that as Christ was raised from the dead by the glory of the Father, we too might walk in newness of life" (CCC 628 [Rom 6:4; cf. Col 2:12; Eph 5:26]).*

*Our Father…*

Lord, as You rose in glory from the tomb, You raise me to new life through Baptism. Help me live out the promises of my baptism in service to You and Your holy Kingdom.

*Hail Mary…*

In rising, You restored our life. When I fear death and doubt rises in my heart, help me be at peace in trusting God, the author of life.

*Hail Mary…*

I can be fearful and bound in my selfishness. By Your cross and Resurrection I have been set free. I will rise in hope to share self-giving love— treating others as I would be treated.

*Hail Mary…*

I am burdened with sorrows. As You awakened the hearts of Your disciples on the road to Emmaus and they found You in the Breaking of the Bread, raise me to find joy in praise and thanksgiving to You.

*Hail Mary…*

After leaving the tomb, Your first visits were to an imperfect woman and an Apostle who denied You. Your mercy seeks us in our brokenness. For those I have hurt, help me seek reconciliation and healing.

*Hail Mary...*

For all who will bury a loved one today and all of the holy souls in Purgatory, may there be hope in anticipation of the resurrection of the body (2 Mac 12:43-46).

*Hail Mary...*

Like reaching into the sea to pull up the doubting Peter, Jesus brought the good news of salvation to the faithful dead. May I join the joyous procession following Him home.

*Hail Mary...*

Christ shows His wounds in His glorified body. Lord, perfect me through my daily sufferings that I may see Your glory beyond my discomfort. May I cherish the wounds won in Your service.

*Hail Mary...*

Mary held Your lifeless body in sorrow and then beheld Your glorified body in rapturous joy. With You, death isn't the end. It is birth from the womb of Earth to eternal life in Heaven.

*Hail Mary...*

Sunday is the day of the Lord. Help me keep it holy.

Hail Mary, full of grace.
The Lord is with thee.
Blessed art thou among women,
and blessed is the fruit of thy womb, Jesus.
Holy Mary, Mother of God, pray for us sinners,
now and at the hour of our death.
Amen.

Glory be to the Father,
to the Son, and
to the Holy Spirit,
as it was, is now, and
ever shall be, world without end.
Amen.


O my Jesus, forgive us our sins,
save us from the fires of Hell;
lead all souls to Heaven,
especially those who have
most need of your mercy.

Spiritual Fruit: Generosity

The Second Glorious Mystery
# Ascension

*"I came from the Father and have come into the world. Now I am leaving the world and going back to the Father." ... "I have told you this so that you might have peace in me. In the world you will have trouble, but take courage, I have conquered the world"* (John 16:28, 33). ... *"Go, therefore, and make disciples of all the nations, baptizing them in the name of the Father and of the Son and of the holy Spirit, teaching them to follow all that I commanded you. And behold, I am with you always, until the end of the age"* (Matt 28:18-20).

*After this event the Apostles became witnesses of the "kingdom [that] will have no end" (CCC 664 [Nicene Creed]). "Christ... fulfills this prophetic office, not only by the hierarchy... but also by the laity. He accordingly both establishes them as witnesses and provides them with the sense of the faith... and the grace of the word" [LG 35]. "To teach in order to lead others to faith is the task of every preacher and of each believer" (CCC 904 [St. Thomas Aquinas, STh. III, 71, 4 ad 3]).*

*Our Father…*

Lord, You spent 40 days after Your Resurrection to Your Ascension teaching Your Apostles (Acts 1:3). Help me learn and trust in the Deposit of Faith You gave the Church. I will hold fast to the Traditions handed down to me (2 Thess 2:15).

*Hail Mary…*

When I feel unloved, I will remember that love is given… I will choose to love more. Help me in word and deed to evangelize the people You have given me to love.

*Hail Mary…*

You went to prepare a place for me. Help me prepare a place for You in my heart and soul. Give me the joy of salvation today and all days.

*Hail Mary…*

*Christ's Ascension marks the definitive entrance of Jesus' humanity into God's heavenly domain…* (CCC 665). As true God and true man, You sanctified our humanity in Yourself. Washed clean in Your blood (Rev 7:14), may I enter Your feast.

*Hail Mary…*

You told the Apostles to convert the nations and then left. We are Your hands and feet continuing Your work in the world. Help me faithfully do my small part with great love.

*Hail Mary...*

Mary's words echo from Cana to the Church after the Ascension: "do whatever He tells you." Lord, help me persevere in daily offerings of prayer, self-denial, and charity.

*Hail Mary...*

Through an active prayer life, daily contemplation of the Word, and frequent participation in the Sacraments, may I be conformed to You.

*Hail Mary...*

The Angel said, "Why are you standing there looking at the sky?" There is a time for marveling at our Lord and a time for work. May I serve, honor, and love Him through my faith in action.

*Hail Mary...*

Lord, You are the way, the truth, and the life. Help me not deny You by careless thoughts, failing to proclaim what is true, and sinful choices.

*Hail Mary...*

May I faithfully proclaim Your death, O Lord, and profess Your Resurrection until You come again.

Hail Mary, full of grace.
The Lord is with thee.
Blessed art thou among women,
and blessed is the fruit of thy womb, Jesus.
Holy Mary, Mother of God, pray for us sinners,
now and at the hour of our death.
Amen.

Glory be to the Father,
to the Son, and
to the Holy Spirit,
as it was, is now, and
ever shall be, world without end.
Amen.

O my Jesus, forgive us our sins,
save us from the fires of Hell;
lead all souls to Heaven,
especially those who have
most need of your mercy.

Spiritual Fruit: Chastity

The Third Glorious Mystery
# Descent of the Holy Spirit

*"... I will build my church, and the gates of the netherworld shall not prevail against it. I will give you the keys to the kingdom of heaven"* (Matt 16:18-19). *"If you love me, you will keep my commandments. And I will ask the Father, and he will give you another Advocate to be with you always, the Spirit of truth... The Advocate, the holy Spirit that the Father will send in my name— he will teach you everything and remind you of all that [I] told you* (John 14:15-17, 26). *... I betrothed you to one husband to present you as a chaste virgin to Christ* (2 Cor 11:2).

*The Church in this world is the sacrament of salvation, the sign and the instrument of the communion of God and men* (CCC 780). *"The sacred liturgy does not exhaust the entire activity of the Church"* [SC 9]: *it must be preceded by evangelization, faith, and conversion. It can then produce its fruits in the lives of the faithful: new life in the Spirit, involvement in the mission of the Church, and service to her unity* (CCC 1072).

*Our Father…*

May I live in faithful communion with the
one, holy, catholic, and apostolic Church—the
holy Bride who is one in flesh with
Christ Himself (CCC 796).

*Hail Mary…*

Lord, the coming of the Holy Spirit was both
fulfillment of promise and empowerment of Your
Church. May Your holy Bride hear the voice of
the Spirit as She receives and reveals all truth.

*Hail Mary…*

The Bible says that not all of Christ's teaching is
contained in it (John 21:25). The rest is given in
Magisterium through the Holy Spirit and Deposit
of Faith. Help me hear and live the truth.

*Hail Mary…*

Lord, as the Church Militant confronts evil in
our age, grant me the courage to stand with all
who hold fast to Scripture and the constant
teachings of the Church.

*Hail Mary…*

*By his coming, which never ceases, the Holy Spirit causes the world to enter into the "last days," the time of the Church…* (CCC 732). Help me be ready.

*Hail Mary…*

Through the power of the Holy Spirit, the Apostles emerged from their room as bold evangelists and martyrs. Lord, transform me, too, so I may faithfully do Your holy will.

*Hail Mary…*

*"We live by the Spirit"; the more we renounce ourselves, the more we "walk by the Spirit."* (CCC 736 [Gal 5:25; cf. Mt 16:24-26]). Help me let go of all that the world offers and desire holiness… to be separated from a world opposed to You (James 4:4).

*Hail Mary…*

Lord, You promised that the Gates of Hell will not prevail against Your Church (Matt 16:18). Gates are defensive… we should storm the Gates with the Gospel! Give me the grace to boldly praise Your name—especially where It's not welcomed.

*Hail Mary…*

*The fruit of sacramental life is both personal and ecclesial* (CCC 1134). Help me recognize in the Sacraments my participation in the family life of God's household.

*Hail Mary...*

The Holy Spirit is poured out on me at Confirmation. May I share Your heavenly gift as I live in the household of God, which is the Church, the pillar and foundation of truth (1 Tim 3:15).

Hail Mary, full of grace.
The Lord is with thee.
Blessed art thou among women,
and blessed is the fruit of thy womb, Jesus.
Holy Mary, Mother of God, pray for us sinners,
now and at the hour of our death.
Amen.

Glory be to the Father,
to the Son, and
to the Holy Spirit,
as it was, is now, and
ever shall be, world without end.
Amen.


O my Jesus, forgive us our sins,
save us from the fires of Hell;
lead all souls to Heaven,
especially those who have
most need of your mercy.

## Spiritual Fruit: Peace

The Fourth Glorious Mystery
# Assumption

*"Do not let your hearts be troubled. You have faith in God; have faith also in me. In my Father's house there are many dwelling places. If there were not, would I have told you that I am going to prepare a place for you? And if I go and prepare a place for you, I will come back again and take you to myself, so that where I am you also may be"* (John 14:1-3).

*The Most Blessed Virgin Mary, when the course of her earthly life was completed, was taken up body and soul into the glory of heaven, where she already shares in the glory of her Son's Resurrection, anticipating the resurrection of all members of his Body (CCC 974). The Christian who unites his own death to that of Jesus views it as a step towards him and an entrance into everlasting life (CCC 1020).*

*Our Father…*

Mary, you are first among Christians to be raised—body and soul—into heavenly glory. Pray for me to follow your example in life so I may join in your inheritance at death.

*Hail Mary…*

As you trusted in God's plan for you, pray for me to trust in His plan for me.

*Hail Mary…*

I am shaped by what I love. In loving You, Lord, may I keep Your word and do Your will. Come and make Your dwelling with me as I follow in Mary's footsteps of faith.

*Hail Mary…*

Mary, your hope was in God alone. I hope in His mercy now and when I stand before your Son on the day of judgement.

*Hail Mary…*

You love Jesus intimately as a mother to her son. I am united with your holy family in a bond forged in Baptism. I celebrate liturgical seasons and familial remembrances with my brothers and sisters in faith.

*Hail Mary…*

In my great desire for everlasting life, I ask for the prayers of my mother Mary, all of the angels and saints, and my family of faith who accompany me on this journey.

*Hail Mary…*

*Those who die in God's grace and friendship and are perfectly purified live forever with Christ* (CCC 1023). I pray for the holy souls in Purgatory and hope to live and die in God's grace and friendship.

*Hail Mary…*

Mary, you are great because of your relationship with your Son and fidelity to the will of God. May I seek no other greatness.

*Hail Mary…*

*To become the mother of the Savior, "Mary was enriched by God with gifts appropriate to such a role"* (CCC 490 [LG 56]). May I use the gifts God gave me for His divine purpose.

*Hail Mary...*

Through my exile in this valley of tears, the cross I carry is a sign of my loving service, a manifestation of my sins, and my ladder to Heaven. Lord, help me persevere until the day You call me home.

Hail Mary, full of grace.
The Lord is with thee.
Blessed art thou among women,
and blessed is the fruit of thy womb, Jesus.
Holy Mary, Mother of God, pray for us sinners,
now and at the hour of our death.
Amen.

Glory be to the Father,
to the Son, and
to the Holy Spirit,
as it was, is now, and
ever shall be, world without end.
Amen.


O my Jesus, forgive us our sins,
save us from the fires of Hell;
lead all souls to Heaven,
especially those who have
most need of your mercy.

## Spiritual Fruit: Gentleness

The Fifth Glorious Mystery
# Coronation

*Then God's temple in heaven was opened, and the ark of his covenant could be seen in the temple.... A great sign appeared in the sky, a woman clothed with the sun, with the moon under her feet, and on her head a crown of twelve stars* (Rev. 11:19-12:1). *And when the chief Shepherd is revealed, you will receive the unfading crown of glory.* (1 Peter 5:4) *Do you not know that we will judge angels* (1 Cor 6:3)? *"Nevertheless, do not rejoice because the spirits are subject to you, but rejoice because your names are written in Heaven"* (Luke 10:20).

*"Finally, the Immaculate Virgin, preserved free from all stain of original sin, when the course of her earthly life was finished, was taken up body and soul into heavenly glory, and exalted by the Lord as Queen over all things, so that she might be the more fully conformed to her Son, the Lord of lords and conqueror of sin and death"* (CCC 966 [LG 59; cf. Pius XII, Munificentissimus Deus (1950): DS 3903; cf. Rev 19:16]). *Heaven is the blessed community of all who are perfectly incorporated into Christ* (CCC 1026).

*Our Father...*

Mary, you are the Queen Mother of the King and embodiment of His Bride, the Church. Help me recognize in you the fulfillment of all promise.

*Hail Mary...*

*Mary's role in the Church is inseparable from her union with Christ and flows directly from it* (CCC 964). Pray for me, O holy Mother of God, that I may be made worthy of the promises of Christ.

*Hail Mary...*

The *Virgin Mary is the Church's model of faith and charity* (CCC 967). As you gave up your Son for my salvation, may I not be selfish with the blessings bestowed on me.

*Hail Mary...*

*What the Catholic faith believes about Mary is based on what it believes about Christ, and what it teaches about Mary illumines, in turn, its faith in Christ* (CCC 487). This is the time of fulfillment. The reign of God is at hand!

*Hail Mary...*

Among the Apostles, two were Christ-killers. One despaired and was lost. The other repented and served the Kingdom. The past and future are both God's domain. I am not the one to judge myself nor anyone else.

*Hail Mary…*

Lord, in Heaven I will be like You—seeing You as You are (1 John 3:2). May I live my life as an outpouring of love to more fully conform myself to You, who is life-giving Love personified.

*Hail Mary…*

*"Mary's greatness consists in the fact that she wants to magnify God, not herself"* (Pope Benedict XVI). Following her example, may I seek to glorify God in all I do.

*Hail Mary…*

Unnatural worldly pleasures lead to slavery to sin. May I be delivered from every evil and granted peace in my days as I wait in joyful hope for the coming of my Savior, Jesus Christ.

*Hail Mary…*

Lord, help me resist the empty attachments of a world that can never match the fulfillment of Heaven. I will walk humbly with You anticipating the glory of Your Kingdom.

*Hail Mary…*

Through the New Covenant sealed in Your blood, I am part of the royal family of Heaven. We worship with one voice in one universal, ageless liturgy. I rejoice in communion with the angels and my triumphant brothers and sisters, the saints.

Hail Mary, full of grace.
The Lord is with thee.
Blessed art thou among women,
and blessed is the fruit of thy womb, Jesus.
Holy Mary, Mother of God, pray for us sinners,
now and at the hour of our death.
Amen.

*Glory be…*

*Fatima Prayer…*

## Hail, Holy Queen!

Hail, Holy Queen, Mother of mercy, our life, our sweetness, and our hope. To thee do we cry, poor banished children of Eve, to thee do we send up our sighs, mourning and weeping in this valley of tears. Turn then, most gracious advocate, thine eyes of mercy toward us; and after this, our exile, show unto us the blessed fruit of thy womb, Jesus.

O clement, O loving, O sweet Virgin Mary.

Pray for us, O holy Mother of God, that we may be made worthy of the promises of Christ.

Let us pray...

O God, whose only-begotten Son, by His life, death, and resurrection, has purchased for us the rewards of eternal salvation; grant we beseech Thee, that meditating upon these mysteries of the most holy Rosary of the Blessed Virgin Mary, we may *imitate what they contain and obtain what they promise.* Through the same Christ our Lord. Amen.

## Optional Closing Prayers

### Memorare

Remember, O most gracious Virgin Mary,
that never was it known that anyone
who fled to your protection,
implored your help, or sought your intercession,
was left unaided. Inspired by this confidence,
I fly unto you, O Virgin of virgins, my Mother.
To you do I come, before you I stand,
sinful and sorrowful.
O Mother of the Word Incarnate, despise not my
petitions, but in your clemency,
hear and answer me.
Amen.

### The Angelus

Pour forth we beseech Thee, O Lord,
Thy grace into our hearts,
that we to whom the incarnation of Christ,
Thy Son, was made known by the message of an
angel, may by His passion and cross be brought
to the glory of His resurrection,
through the same Christ Our Lord.
Amen.

## Prayer to St Michael the Archangel

St. Michael the Archangel,
defend us in battle.
Be our defense against the
wickedness and snares of the Devil.
May God rebuke him, we humbly pray,
and do thou, O Prince of the heavenly hosts,
by the power of God,
thrust into Hell Satan,
and all the evil spirits,
who prowl about the world
seeking the ruin of souls.
Amen.

## Memorare to St Joseph

Remember, most chaste spouse of the Virgin
Mary, that never was it known that anyone who
implored your help and sought your intercession
were left unassisted. Full of confidence in your
power, I fly unto you and beg your protection.
Despise not, O Guardian of the Redeemer, my
humble supplication but, in your bounty, hear
and answer me.
Amen.

## Prayer to St Joseph after the Rosary

This prayer to Saint Joseph—spouse of the Virgin Mary, foster father of Jesus, and patron saint of the universal Church—was composed by Pope Leo XIII in his 1889 encyclical, *Quamquam Pluries*. He asked that it be added to the end of the Rosary, especially during the month of October, which is dedicated to the Rosary. The prayer is enriched with a partial indulgence (*Handbook of Indulgences*, conc. 19) and may be said after the customary Salve Regina and concluding prayer. (From www.usccb.org)

To you, O blessed Joseph,
do we come in our tribulation, and
having implored the help of your most holy
Spouse, we confidently invoke
your patronage also.

Through that charity which bound you
to the Immaculate Virgin Mother of God
and through the paternal love
with which you embraced the Child Jesus,
we humbly beg you
graciously to regard the inheritance
which Jesus Christ has purchased by his Blood,
and with your power and strength to aid us in our
necessities.

O most watchful guardian of the Holy Family,
defend the chosen children of Jesus Christ;
O most loving father, ward off from us
every contagion of error and corrupting
influence; O our most mighty protector, be kind
to us and from Heaven assist us in our struggle
with the power of darkness.

As once you rescued the Child Jesus
from deadly peril, so now protect God's Holy
Church from the snares of the enemy and from
all adversity; shield, too, each one of us
by your constant protection, so that, supported
by your example and your aid,
we may be able to live piously, to die in holiness,
and to obtain eternal happiness in Heaven.
Amen.

## Prayer for The Eternal Rest

Eternal rest grant unto them, O Lord, and let
perpetual light shine upon them. May the souls
of all the faithful departed,
through the mercy of God, rest in peace.

## A Prayer for the Souls in Purgatory
By Saint Gertrude

Eternal Father,
I offer Thee the most precious Blood
of Thy Divine Son, Jesus,
in union with the Masses said
throughout the world today,
for all the holy souls in Purgatory,
for sinners everywhere,
for sinners in the universal Church,
those in my own home
and within my family.
Amen.

**Protoevangelium:** *After his fall, man was not abandoned by God. On the contrary, God calls him and in a mysterious way heralds the coming victory over evil and his restoration from his fall* [Cf. Gen 3:9, 15]. *This passage in Genesis is called the* Protoevangelium *("first gospel"): the first announcement of the Messiah and Redeemer, of a battle between the serpent and the Woman, and of the final victory of a descendant of hers* (CCC 410).

**Fruits of the Spirit**: *The* fruits *of the Spirit are perfections that the Holy Spirit forms in us as the first fruits of eternal glory* (CCC 1832).

**Faithfulness**: Faith is the core of Christianity. Faithfulness means living according to the will of God and believing that He is the master of life.

**Kindness**: Kindness is more than simply "being kind" to others. It is having a heart that is willing to do acts of compassion and give to others above and beyond what we owe to them.

**Goodness**: Goodness can be a euphemism for God Himself. ... *"Good teacher, what must I do to inherit eternal life?" Jesus answered him, "Why do you call me good? No one is good but God alone"* (Luke 18:18-19). In His great love for us, God gives us Himself.

**Patience**: Patience can be understood as hopeful waiting. It also comes from an understanding of our own imperfect state and how God has given us His unconditional love and mercy. As God is patient with our faults and failings, we share the same patience for the faults of others.

**Modesty**: We should give God and neighbor the reverence deserved... and treat human bodies as the temples God made them to be. Modesty is an antonym to pride. It implies humility and service. It is obedience to the will of God.

**Joy**: The joy that comes from the Spirit is more than an emotional state. It is a lasting happiness that can only be realized when we put God at the center of our lives in the belief that we will live our eternal life with Him.

**Generosity**: Generosity is giving more than just physical resources. We, as people of God, are required to go beyond our own needs for the needs of the Church and others. This generosity often takes the form of time, talent, and treasure.

**Chastity**: While usually viewed in the context of sexual appetites, chastity also implies fidelity to the bonds and responsibilities of covenantal marriage. It is the keeping of each solely for one another as the proper condition of marital love. It is mutual faithfulness. In chastity, we love and faithfully serve God alone.

**Peace**: In complete trust and reliance on God, we have a tranquility that comes from believing that He will provide for us now and forever. Peace relieves us from anxious thoughts about the future.

**Gentleness**: Far from weakness, gentleness requires strength. A weak person may require a great deal of effort to be forceful while a strong person uses only a fraction of his strength. A light touch from one who is powerful is gentleness.

**Cardinal Virtues**: *Four virtues play a pivotal role and accordingly are called "cardinal"; all the others are grouped around them* (CCC 1805).

> **Prudence**: *It is prudence that immediately guides the judgment of conscience. The prudent man determines and directs his conduct in accordance with this judgment. With the help of this virtue we apply moral principles to particular cases without error and overcome doubts about the good to achieve and the evil to avoid* (CCC 1806). Prudence is the firm resolve to do the will of God.

> **Justice**: The *moral virtue that consists in the constant and firm will to give their due to God and neighbor* (CCC 1807). Justice is accepting the full measure of recompense in obedience to God.

> **Temperance**: The *moral virtue that moderates the attraction of pleasures and provides balance in the use of created goods. It ensures the will's mastery over instincts and keeps desires within the limits of what is honorable* (CCC 1809). Temperance is a king meekly accepting scorn and ridicule in obedience to God.

**Fortitude**: The *moral virtue that ensures firmness in difficulties and constancy in the pursuit of the good. It strengthens the resolve to resist temptations and to overcome obstacles in the moral life. The virtue of fortitude enables one to conquer fear, even fear of death, and to face trials and persecutions* (CCC 1808). Fortitude is marching forward—even toward destruction—in obedience to God.

**Charity**: *By charity, we love God above all things and our neighbor as ourselves for love of God. Charity, the form of all the virtues, "binds everything together in perfect harmony"* (CCC 1844 [Col 3:14]). Charity is perfect self-giving and sacrificial love.

# THE PERSONAL ROSARY

This page is available for your personal
notes, thoughts, and reflections.